REA

# The Mysterious & Unknown

# Angels

## by Stuart A. Kallen

ReferencePoint
Press™

San Diego, CA

**For more information, contact:**
ReferencePoint Press, Inc.
PO Box 27779
San Diego, CA 92198
www.ReferencePointPress.com

Picture credits:
cover: iStockphoto.com
Maury Aaseng: 9
AP Images: 43
iStockphoto.com: 19, 28, 36, 47
Landov: 12
Dan Leone: 22
North Wind: 8, 16, 45, 50, 54–55, 60, 75, 84, 92
Photos.com: 6, 63, 69


Series design and book layout:
Amy Stirnkorb

LIBRARY OF CONGRESS CATALOGING-IN-PUBLICATION DATA

Kallen, Stuart A., 1955–
Angels by Stuart A. Kallen.
  p. cm. (Mysterious & unknown)
  Includes bibliographical references and index.

  ISBN-13: 978-1-60152-055-5 (hardback)
  ISBN-10: 1-60152-055-7 (hardback)
  1. Angels. I. Title.
  BL477.K35 2008

  202'.15--dc22                                                    2008019671

# CONTENTS

# FOREWORD

"Strange is our situation here upon earth."
—*Albert Einstein*

Since the beginning of recorded history, people have been perplexed, fascinated, and even terrified by events that defy explanation. While science has demystified many of these events, such as volcanic eruptions and lunar eclipses, some remain outside the scope of the provable. Do UFOs exist? Are people abducted by aliens? Can some people see into the future? These questions and many more continue to puzzle, intrigue, and confound despite the enormous advances of modern science and technology.

It is these questions, phenomena, and oddities that Reference-Point Press's *The Mysterious & Unknown* series is committed to exploring. Each volume examines historical and anecdotal evidence as well as the most recent theories surrounding the topic in debate. Fascinating primary source quotes from scientists, experts, and eyewitnesses as well as in-depth sidebars further inform the text. Full-color illustrations and photos add to each book's visual appeal. Finally, source notes, a bibliography, and a thorough index provide further reference and research support. Whether for research or the curious reader, *The Mysterious & Unknown* series is certain to satisfy those fascinated by the unexplained.

# Introduction

# Attracted to Angels

In 1983 Joan Wester Anderson was nervously waiting for her son to arrive home for Christmas. Tim was driving from Connecticut to Chicago, and the weather was bitterly cold with temperatures dipping to 30 degrees below zero. It was after midnight, a blinding snow was blowing, and Tim was 5 hours late. Unfortunately, Tim's car had broken down about 100 miles (161km) from home on a lonely stretch of road in Indiana. The young man was sure he was about to freeze to death. Although Anderson was unaware of her son's situation she began to pray like she never had before. "God, you've got to send someone. Please send someone. Because I don't think I can bear what might be happening here. So send someone."[1] Moments later, in Indiana, the bright lights of a tow truck appeared in Tim's rearview mirror. A man got out and offered his help. Anderson's son clambered into the warm cab of the tow truck as the driver hitched up the frozen car. After towing him to safety, the man and his truck

simply disappeared before Tim could pay him. They did not even leave tracks in the snow.

When Tim finally greeted his mother in Chicago the next day, he told her of the odd experience. After discussing the details, the Andersons realized that the tow truck driver showed up a little after 1:00 A.M., moments after Joan had prayed. In the months that followed, Joan tried to track down the mysterious tow truck driver but failed. She soon came to believe that it was an angel who saved her son.

Anderson is a journalist. After what she calls her son's angelic interference, she began collecting angel stories from others. Since that time, Anderson has written 15 best-selling books about angelic interference and has appeared on national television programs, including *Good Morning America, Oprah,* and *20/20.*

Anderson's books are part of a massive angel craze that began in the late 1980s. This fad has generated countless publications, Web sites, and magazine articles that feature stories of supposed real-life encounters with angels.

*Opposite page: These angels help ring church bells. All religions teach that angels exist. They are not the spirits of the dead, like ghosts, but supernatural, nonhuman beings that act as messengers or warriors of God.*

## Angels Are Everywhere

All religions, including Judaism, Christianity, Buddhism, Hinduism, and Islam teach that angels exist. They are not the spirits of the dead, like ghosts, but supernatural, nonhuman beings that act as messengers or warriors of God. In the Bible God's angels do battle with dragons, help Peter escape from prison, and use flashing swords to guard the Gates of Eden.

Biblical appearances of angels are mainly connected to important events, such as the birth of Jesus or the battle between good and evil at the end of the world. In recent decades, however, angelic interference seems to have become commonplace. Modern believers say angels can influence nearly every aspect of life and death. It is said angels can be consulted to solve mundane

*This girl sleeps soundly as her guardian angel watches over her. Some people believe that they have their own individual supernatural entities, like guardian angels, that travel with them everywhere.*

problems with family relationships, love affairs, and business decisions. They can avert disasters, help heal the sick, allow people to talk to the dead, or even provide a way to see into the future. If the published stories are true, angels are everywhere all the time. And they can help anyone and everyone in a crisis. Little wonder then that a vast majority of Americans have faith that angels are real. In a 2004 Gallup poll 78 percent of adults said they believe in the existence of angels. Fifty percent believe that they have their own guardian angel to look over them. And 30 percent said they have had personal encounters with angels.

The angel fad, rather than religious belief, has undoubtedly helped increase the poll numbers. The number of people who say they believe in angels is about twice the number of those who say they attend religious services every week. But in times of economic difficulty, terrorism, and war, angels have helped people deal with the uncertainties of life. And if polls are to be believed, 90 million Americans have been helped by supernatural angel power. Those people and other believers have little doubt that humans are not alone on Earth. Instead they are surrounded by heavenly creatures who care deeply about their health, happiness, and material comforts.

# Most Americans Believe in Angels

Americans say they believe in heaven more than hell. More say they believe in God than say they believe in the devil. Seventy-five percent of Americans believe in angels.

| | Believe in | Not sure | Don't believe in |
|---|---|---|---|
| God | 86% | 8% | 6% |
| Heaven | 81% | 8% | 11% |
| Angels | 75% | 11% | 14% |
| Devil | 70% | 8% | 21% |
| Hell | 69% | 8% | 22% |

# Belief in Angels Declining Slightly

In 2001 belief in angels was at 79 percent. Since then, belief in angels has decreased slightly.

| | Believe in | Not sure | Don't believe in | No opinion |
|---|---|---|---|---|
| 2007 | 75% | 11% | 14% | * |
| 2004 | 78% | 11% | 10% | 1% |
| 2001 | 79% | 12% | 8% | 1% |
| 1996 | 72% | 11% | 16% | 1% |
| 1994 | 72% | 13% | 15% | * |

* less than 0.5%

Source: Gallup Poll, "Americans More Likely to Believe in God than the Devil, Heaven More than Hell," June 13, 2007. www.gallup.com.

# CHAPTER 1

# In the Beginning

Angels are mentioned in the Old Testament, the New Testament, the Koran, and other holy books. But the first known pictures of angels are literally carved into stone. Ancient Sumerians, who lived in present-day Iraq, sculpted angels onto stone tablets about 5,000 years ago. The word *angel* means "messenger" in Greek, and the ancient Sumerian angel was a messenger of God. It had come down from heaven to pour the water of life into a king's cup.

The Sumerians believed that people had their own individual supernatural entities, like guardian angels, that traveled with them everywhere. These protective spirits, known as *kuribi,* are pictured with human heads, birdlike wings, and animal bodies.

Each Sumerian had an altar in his or her home to honor their personal kuribi, and these beings were the focus of poetry, paintings, and religious teachings.

In this era before monotheism, or the belief in a single god, many cultures applied angelic qualities to their gods and goddesses. In ancient Egypt, around 2500 B.C., the mother goddess Isis and the goddess of justice, Maat, were considered helpful winged spirits. The Egyptians, who believed in about 1,200 different deities, also thought that angelic spirits visited the dead. To accommodate these angels, the Egyptians built elaborate tombs with small windows for angels to enter.

## Angelology

Angel spirits appeared in drawings and carvings for thousands of years. However, the first written reference to angels originated in Persia, or present-day Iran. Around 1000 B.C. the Zoroastrians developed a complex belief system based on angels called angelology. The Zoroastrians believe that their prophet Zarathushtra, or Zoroaster, was guided by six chief angels, called archangels. These angelic messengers helped Zoroaster meet Ahura Mazda, the supreme lord of the universe. With the help of the angels, Zoroaster was also able to communicate with Ahura Mazda, who gave the prophet wisdom.

The first archangel to appear to Zoroaster was Vohumanah, or Good Thoughts. This angel is nine times bigger than a man and acts as the presiding lord of domestic animals. Vohumanah gave Zoroaster the power to step out of his physical body and enter the realm of Ahura Mazda in heaven. Another archangel, Asha Vahishta, is called the spirit of righteousness and lord of sacred

Angels are mentioned in the Old Testament, the New Testament, the Koran, and other holy books.

The Egyptians worshipped Isis, the mother goddess. In the era before monotheism, or the belief in a single god, many cultures applied angelic qualities to their gods and goddesses. In ancient Egypt, around 2500 B.C., Isis was considered a helpful winged spirit.

fires. This spirit ordered Zoroaster to protect the sacred divine fire and all other fires that warm people on Earth.

Zoroaster met other archangels that represented plants, the soil, metals, and waters. Together these archangels are called Amesha Spenta. They represent different aspects of Ahura Mazda and act as the foundation of the universe.

The Amesha Spenta have their own angels who assist them. There are 23 of these beings, called Yazata, or "worthy of worship," and Yazad, or "divine." Various aspects of these angels watch over divine wisdom, victory, charity, peace, health, riches, cattle, happiness, and morality.

Another rank of Zoroastrian angelology describes guardian angels who act as guides and protectors. Zoroaster described this type of angel as "a strong and watchful warrior who wears armor and carries weapons."[2]

Zoroastrians also believe that a class of angels are evil and act as demons. For example, Ahriman represents wickedness, and this devil tried to kill Zoroaster after his first visit with Ahura Mazda. However, the prophet's spiritual powers allowed him to conquer Ahriman.

Zoroastrians believe that good angels will someday go into battle with bad angels. After the cataclysmic combat, individuals will be judged as either worthy or sinful and unworthy by the divine spirit.

## Hebrew Angels

The idea of angel warriors punishing the sinful found its way into the Jewish Bible, or Old Testament. The earliest Hebrew scholars believed that God spoke directly to humans and intervened in their affairs, destroying sinners without mercy. However, the Hebrews

Five thousand years
ago, the ancient
Sumerians believed
that people had
their own individual
guardian angels who
traveled with them
everywhere.

later adapted aspects of Zoroastrian angelology. They made God more merciful but distant from humanity. In his place, righteous angels judge peoples' deeds and meted out punishment. Demons, or evil angels, took on destructive powers.

In the Old Testament, angels are referred to variously as sons of God, divine beings, holy ones, watchers, and the host of heaven. And the functions of the angels are as varied as their descriptions. Angels make up a heavenly court that surrounds God. There they sings his praises and serve as an army of a thousand warriors. As messengers, angels announce births, commission various people to engage in divine tasks, and communicate God's words to prophets. Angels also act as teachers and heavenly guides, interpreting prophecies and explaining holy visions. These biblical angels are creatures of incredible beauty. They appear as brilliant beams of light, blazing fires, shiny metal, or precious stones. In some cases they have wings, human features, and circles of light, or halos, around their heads.

The most powerful angels of the Old Testament are archangels, or chief angels, who act as liaisons between humans and God. Four archangels are mentioned in the Old Testament. Michael is the warrior of heaven, and Gabriel is the heavenly messenger. Raphael is God's healer or helper, and Uriel watches over the world and the lowest part of hell.

## "Each Had the Face of a Man"

Cherubim, or cherubs, are the second most powerful angels in the Old Testament and are mentioned 91 times. The word "cherub" comes from the Hebrew *kerubh,* meaning "fullness of knowledge" or "one who intercedes." These angels who intervene in human affairs are the first angels mentioned in the Bible. In the book of Genesis cherubim are placed at the entrance to the Garden of Eden to prevent Adam and Eve from returning. However, the first physical description of cherubim is given by Ezekiel, who has a fantastic vision of the angels carrying the throne of God. According to Ezekiel 1:5–11:

> Within [the vision] there were figures resembling four living beings. And this was their appearance: they had human form.
>
> Each of them had four faces and four wings.
>
> Their legs were straight and their feet were like a calf's hoof, and they gleamed like burnished bronze.
>
> Under their wings on their four sides were human hands. As for the faces and wings of the four of them, their wings touched one another; their faces did not turn when they moved, each went straight forward.
>
> As for the form of their faces, each had the face of a man; all four had the face of a lion on the right and the face of a bull on the left, and all four had the face of an eagle.
>
> Such were their faces. Their wings were spread out above; each had two touching another being, and two covering their bodies.

*A cherub escorts Adam and Eve out of the Garden of Eden after they sin. These angels, who intervene in human affairs, are the first angels mentioned in the Bible.*

Ezekiel sees the angels by the River Chebar in a great cloud of flashing fire. Besides the angels, four wheels with spokes that seem like wheels within wheels appear. The cherubim and the wheels seem to move in all directions at once, amid lightning and thunder. After speaking to God on the throne, Ezekiel ascends to heaven and sees the cherubim once again.

## As Big as Heaven

Angels that have even more power than cherubim are called seraphim. These angels are based on the Zoroastrian angels of fire—the word *seraphim* loosely translates from Hebrew as "burn," "incinerate," or "destroy." And when the seraphim appear in the Bible, burning and destruction are sure to follow.

In the book of Numbers a fiery seraph, in the form of a snake, bites and kills Israelite sinners. However, the prophet Isaiah sees seraphim in a more human form, attending the throne of God. The creatures have 6 wings, 2 to shield their faces from the brilliant light of God, 2 to shield their feet, and 2 used for flying.

Apocalyptic Hebrew writings of about 200 B.C.–A.D. 150 called the book of Enoch give a detailed description of 4 seraphim, representing the 4 winds or north, south, east, and west. Each seraph has 16 faces, 4 facing in each direction. The faces are as bright as the rising sun, and the light is so intense that even other angels, such as cherubim, cannot look upon it. Each seraph has 6 wings that represent the 6 days of Earth's creation. And each wing is as big as heaven.

The book of Enoch states that seraphim also interact with Satan, a fallen angel whose name translates as "adversary," "opponent," or "obstacle" in Hebrew. According to the text, Satan sits down every day and writes out the sins of Israel on tablets. The fallen angel then gives these tablets to seraphim to take to God in the hope that God will destroy Israel for its sins. However, the seraphim know God does not want to do this, so they burn Satan's tablets and protect Israel.

## Angel Adversaries

Despite his task against the Israelites, the Hebrews did not originally consider Satan the embodiment of all evil. Instead, the term *satan* is

The ancient Hebrews
believed righteous
angels judged
peoples' deeds
and meted out
punishment, while
demons, or evil
angels, took on
destructive powers.

used to describe a variety of angels. These figures obstruct or oppose human activity and act as adversaries against humans. However, the angels called Satan do not act against God. For example, in the book of Job, an angelic Satan works as a prosecutor in the court of justice against men who displeased or disobeyed God.

As centuries passed, Israelites began using the term *satan* for human enemies who persecuted them. As a result, the angels came to be characterized as a single fallen angel, or one who was evicted from heaven. In the guise of evil personified, Satan came to be associated with other fallen angels such as Beelzebub, Semyaza, and Azazel.

Around 2,000 years ago, the angel Satan was transformed into the ruler of hell in the Christian New Testament. In this new role, Satan is identified as the enemy of humanity, the tempter, the father of lies and murder, and the serpent. To carry out his wicked deeds, he acts as the leader of demons who oppose God and Jesus. He hinders the work of Jesus's believers and slanders and persecutes them with the ferocity of a lion. He is able to do this by using supernatural powers that can destroy all of humanity through sin.

## Angelic Revelations

The New Testament defines the archangel Michael as one who can defend the world against the forces of Satanic darkness. As a result, Michael is a saint in the Catholic religion.

Many other angels appear in the New Testament, and most act as ministers of God and agents of revelation, particularly concerning Jesus. The archangel Gabriel, for example, appears to Mary as a traditional angelic messenger, informing her that the child in her womb is Jesus, the son of God. Other angels are there to herald the birth of Jesus, witness his ascent into heaven, and prophesy his return.

Perhaps the most dramatic role angels play in the New Testament is in the fight to establish good and vanquish evil. This graphic confrontation is described in Revelation, the last book of the New Testament. It foretells the coming of Jesus, the end of the world, the Last Judgment, and the establishment of a new heaven on Earth. Sinners are punished, and the righteous are rewarded in a new heavenly city.

The book of Revelation, also known as the Revelation of John, begins with angels delivering a message from God. Throughout the 22 chapters of Revelation, angels

*Beelzebub (in water), seen here with Satan, is a fallen angel who was expelled from heaven. He is Satan's chief demon. Beelzebub is said to have powers only second to Satan's. In heaven he was the highest-ranking angel.*

are central to the spectacular events as they unfold. In chapter 8:5, 7 angels with 7 trumpets wreak havoc on Earth. One angel fills a censer with fire and throws it down to Earth causing lightning, thunder, and earthquakes. This is followed by "hail and fire

# Beyond Merely Human

Hindu devas are protective godlike angels. On the Hinduism Today Web site, religious teacher Swami Sivasiva Palani describes the duties of devas in small villages:

> In folk Hinduism [angels called] "village gods" are important. These are often called kshetrapala "protectors of the field or place." They watch the land, keeping intruders away, and they are often set up in the northeastern corner of the farm or village, facing east, with their all-seeing three eyes and their manifold arms dis-

mingled with blood . . . and the third part of trees was burnt up, and all green grass was burnt up." This angel also caused the sea to flow red with blood and a star to fall and burn up rivers.

In Revelation 8:12, a fourth angel sounded his trumpet, and the sun was smitten as well as the moon and the stars. Later, seven playing protective powers. Many are females, worshipped widely for protection, often associated with the color blue, and said to be guardians of pools, lakes and plants. . . . There are angels that oversee marriage, fertility and health. Those that protect the home and the hamlet. Those that bring messages and warn of dangers. Those that run with animals and inspire music. There are [devas] that harm and injure, communicate disease and wreak havoc. In short, every human activity has its spiritual, devonic dimension which lies beyond the merely human.

Sivasiva Palani, "New Angels on Angels," *Hinduism Today*, 2008. www.hinduism today.com.

angels bring seven plagues to Earth, and the archangel Michael fights Satan and commands angel warriors in a final conflict between good and evil.

In the last chapters of Revelation, angels show John a new holy city on Earth where the river of life flows crystal clear. Revelation 22:16

**Angels**

ends with the statement that highlights the importance of angels in this final chapter of the Christian Bible: "I, Jesus, have sent my angel to make these revelations to you for the sake of the church."

## Angels of Islam

About six centuries after the New Testament ended with angelic revelations, the Koran was written based on the words of an archangel. People of the Islamic faith believe that around A.D. 610, the archangel Gabriel revealed God's messages to the prophet Muhammad. The prophet recorded these revelations in the Koran over the course of 23 years. When the message was finalized, Islam spread rapidly across the Middle East and Central Asia. As with Christianity and Judaism, angels play a major role.

Islamic angelology is based on a hierarchy, or ranking, of angels. The top angels are most important as throne bearers of Allah, or God. They are symbolized by a man, a bull, an eagle, and a lion. The next order of angels consists of cherubim who praise Allah. The next order down consists of four archangels: Jibril, or Gabriel, the revealer; Mikal, or Michael, the provider; 'Izra'il, the angel of death; and Israfil, the angel of the Last Judgment.

Lesser angels known as *hafazah* or *hafza* are guardian angels. The Koran also describes recording angels. Two of these angels are assigned to every human being to observe and write down their actions. This is stated in Sura Qaf, 16–18: "We created man and We know what his own self whispers to him. We are nearer to him than his jugular vein. And the two recording angels are recording, sitting on the right and on the left. He does not utter a single word, without a watcher by him, pen in hand!"

Angels also place souls in newborn babies and oversee the rains and the growth of plants. When people die, angels take their souls.

*Opposite page: This statue shows the arch-angel Michael defeating the serpent. The New Testament defines Michael as one who can defend the world against the forces of Satanic darkness.*

## Created from Liquid Fire

The angels of the Koran are created from light and possess amazing beauty. For example, Gabriel is said to have 600 wings. But most Islamic angels do not possess free will, and they are unable to disobey Allah. However, a type of supernatural spirit, low-level angels called jinn, djinn, or genies possess free will. Jinn are created from liquid fire, have powers to assume animal, insect, or human form, and can influence people in both positive and negative ways.

It is said that the original jinn were created as equals to angels 2,000 years before the birth of Adam. Their ruler was named Eblis. When Allah created Adam, Eblis refused to bow before the lowly human being. When Allah asked why, Eblis replied, according to Sura 7:12, "I am better than he; Thou created me out of fire and him, Thou created out of clay." This displeased Allah who degraded the status of Eblis and cast him from heaven along with the other jinn. Angered by his fallen status, Eblis swore to tempt Adam and all his sons to see if they would forever remain true to Allah. Anyone who strayed off God's path and followed Eblis would be sent to hell. In this role, Eblis became the king of the evil demons called *shaitans*, or *satans*. This type of jinn is sworn to lead humans into sin by temptation.

Not all jinn are wicked. The invisible wish-granting genie described in many ancient Arabic folktales performs magical rites that help humans satisfy their desires. These low-level angels can travel across the globe instantly and appear anywhere. According to the Koran, genies were created from smokeless fire and have no bodies but can appear in many forms through the use of illusion. In their many guises, genies can appear as snakes, dogs, black cats, or toads. They are said to be as plentiful as grains of sand and cause shooting stars and violent sandstorms.

One of the most famous genies is described in the tale of Aladdin in *A Thousand and One Arabian Nights.* This genie appears when the poor boy Aladdin rubs a magic lamp. The angel is obligated to grant Aladdin's wishes, and the boy becomes a rich and powerful ruler.

## Hindu Angels

While angels are central to Jewish, Christian, and Islamic belief, they play a smaller role in Hinduism. Instead, Hindus believe that gods and goddesses do the type of work that is assigned to angels in the Bible and Koran. As Hindu holy man Guru Maharaji states: "In India people don't see angels. They see Gods."[3]

While not as prominent in people's affairs, many supernatural creatures with angelic qualities are described in Hindu scriptures. These are called *devas, devatas,* or *vandevatas. Deva* means "shining one," and these supernatural creatures are said to live in every tree and by every river crossing. Belief in devas is so strong that religious villagers will not cut down old trees because they fear disturbing the devas that live within them.

Devas are similar to guardian angels and act as sentinels over every field and town. People set up shrines for them along roadsides, near wells, and in caves and mountains. And these spirits watch over almost every aspect of life. Carpenters believe in a deva known as Tachakali who helps them saw, hammer, drill, and build. Women build shrines to the deva Periathambiran near their laundry ponds to help ease their difficult chores. And musicians, truck drivers, and weavers all have their own devas to guide them. In fact 33 million different devas, each with a unique function, are said to exist. Religious teacher Swami Sivasiva Palani describes the ubiquitous presence of devas: "[You] can't step on a rock, enter a house or work in the garden

without an awareness of them. Devas occupy every scripture, every temple, every sacred icon. They attend the dawn and hover at dusk. Like God Himself, they are everywhere, these sacred presences."[4]

## Evil Devas

Hindus also believe in evil spirits called *asuras,* a word meaning "power-hungry." Like angels and demons in Judeo-Christian belief, asuras are evil devas that wage war against good devas. The asuras appear in various forms, including small, mischievous goblins and cruel giants. They symbolize evil, darkness, and drought. However, in one of the most dramatic Hindu stories the good and bad spirits work together.

In the story known as the churning of the milk, or Samudra manthan, devas and asuras join forces to create the nectar of immortality. On the suggestion of Brahma, the god of creation, asuras are advised to churn the ocean until it becomes milk. Such a huge task cannot be undertaken by the asuras alone, so they join forces with their enemies the asuras. Using the King of Snakes, Vasuki, as a rope and Mount Mandara as the churn, the devas and asuras begin their task. The asuras pull on Vasuki's head while the devas pull on his tail. As the mountain rotates, the ocean is churned into milk.

After first conjuring up a deadly poison, they finally create the nectar of immortality. However, the asuras rush to steal it from the angels. After many battles, the nectar is finally returned to the devas.

Only one asura, Rahu, managed to drink the nectar, but his head was cut off before he could swallow it. However, Rahu's head remains immortal and he occasionally swallows the sun or moon, causing eclipses. After the sun or moon passes through his neck, it returns to its proper place in the sky.

## Thirty-six Million Years Old

Like Hinduism, Buddhism has roots in ancient India. And Buddhists, like Hindus, believe in numerous godlike angels called devas.

Buddhist devas are usually invisible. However, persons who develop mystical extrasensory powers can see and hear the angels. And sometimes devas assume various forms to make themselves visible to average people.

All devas are made of light, but those of higher rank possess abilities not available to lower-level devas. The high-ranking spirits can fly through the air, traveling effortlessly across the planet. These devas do not need to eat and drink to survive. Those of the lower ranks can travel only by using magical flying chariots and require food or water like humans.

One class of devas, Arupadhatu, have no body and live in a formless world separate from the universe. Devas called Rupadhatu live in heavenly realms called deva worlds that exist in layers above Earth. These angelic creatures live in various states of bliss and tranquility. Some are the spirits of people who have died before they attain a state of religious enlightenment. Brahma devas, who live in this realm, interact with humanity and offer people advice on spiritual matters.

In the complex angelology of Buddhism exists a world called Kamadhatu that floats above the mythical Mount Sumeru said to exist at the center of the world. This place contains high-level devas that look like humans but are larger and live longer. These angels are happy and are unaware of the discord that exists on Earth. However, lower devas of Kamadhatu are temperamental. While they are passionate and joyful, sometimes their passions lead to aggressive and hostile behavior.

Another part of Kamadhatu is known as the world of

### Did You Know?

Hindus believe in guardian angels called devas that watch over humanity.

*Gabriel is depicted in the stained glass of a church window. Angels are commonly depicted in stained glass windows and other religious architecture.*

33 devas. This area above Mount Sumeru contains palaces and gardens. The 33 devas are 1,500 feet (457m) tall and live 36 million years. They are attended by other supernatural creatures, lower-level devas and nymphs that take care of their needs.

It is said that human beings once possessed the powers of the devas. They could fly, shone brightly with an inner light, and did not require food. However, after consuming food, their bodies grew coarse, and their angelic powers slipped away.

**"QUOTE"**

"[You] can't step on a rock, enter a house or work in the garden without an awareness of them. Devas occupy every scripture, every temple, every sacred icon."

—Swami Sivasiva Palani, explaining the ubiquitous presence of angel-like devas.

## Angels Unite People

Angelology is often complicated. But angels of the world's major religions possess many similar characteristics. And belief in angels is widespread in every country and populated continent on Earth. Whether they are inventions of the human imagination or cosmic creations beyond understanding, angelology is nearly universal. As beautiful beings of light that emanate wisdom and divine messages, angels unite people in the belief that good always triumphs over evil.

# CHAPTER 2

# The Lives of Angels

Angels have been depicted in books and art for thousands of years. They have assumed human form in ancient stone tablets, Renaissance paintings, and countless stories. People have described in detail what angels look like, how they act, what they do, and where they live. Much of this information is based on purported eyewitness accounts, interpretations of holy books, and artistic inspiration.

The modern image of a winged angel with human features is largely based on ideas first developed in the early 1200s. Around that time, human interaction with angels seemed to increase, especially in Italy. Medieval writers such as St. Bonaventure and St. Gregory told of wondrous encounters with seraphim and other angels. Reports of these divine meetings inspired religious scholars to investigate the nature and characteristics of angels, which were not often clearly defined in the Bible. As author David Keck explains in *Angels and Angelology in the Middle Ages*, theologians wanted to know, "What [exactly] do angels look like? Do they have bodies? How would medieval Christians imagine an angel? Do they have personalities and emotions? How many of these creatures are there?"[5]

The interest in angel behavior coincided with a growing interest in science and learning. Religious scholars were redefining biblical knowledge using recently developed ideas about geography and mathematics. This allowed them to map out heaven and hell and apply precise ranks and numbers to the angelic choirs.

## The Angelic Doctor

Italian priest Thomas Aquinas was one of the leading scholars of angelology. His work on the subject was so important that 50 years after his death in 1274 he was canonized as a saint. Nearly three centuries later he was named *Doctor Angelicus,* or the "Angelic Doctor," by Pope Pius V.

During his life St. Thomas achieved widespread renown describing the personalities, activities, and physical characteristics of angels. He used reason and logic to argue that angels were governed by the laws of the universe. To St. Thomas, angelology was as precise and natural as the movement of the sun, stars, and planets through the heavens.

St. Thomas describes angels in a massive treatise called the *Summa Theologica.* This book features complex tracts on subjects such as the nature of God, creation, angels, human nature, happiness, and virtue. In a section called "Celestial Hierarchy of Dionysius" St. Thomas describes and defines nine ranks of angels based on writings by theologians from earlier centuries. He elaborated on this intricate hierarchy in lectures at the University of Paris. These talks attracted huge crowds and were known to last for days. They were also written down by scribes and form the foundation for Christian angelology today.

Using techniques of logic developed by the Greek philosopher Aristotle, St. Thomas attempted to prove the existence of angels. He describes them as God's perfect creations, each one a single species to itself, each one as individual as a snowflake. And according to St. Thomas, angels, like snowflakes, are so numerous that they cannot be counted. In their perfection they cannot die, decay, or change. They can assume human form. But they do not function as humans beings, who are guided by their senses and their intellect. Angels obtain their knowledge directly from God upon creation, and they radiate love and light.

According to St. Thomas, angels do not influence humans by speaking to them. Angels are messengers for God but their speech does not contain sounds or words. Instead, angels conjure up images in the human mind. These vivid mind pictures inspire people to follow God's will. In this way angels serve as divine instruments with the power to work miracles.

## Angel Rankings

The Bible gives the names of nine groups of angels but does not specify their ranks or heavenly duties. St. Thomas used his extensive knowledge of the Bible and the writings of earlier theologians to arrange the angels into three groups called triads or hierarchies. Each hierarchy is broken down into three orders or choirs. The position of the angel in the hierarchy determines its jobs, the length of time it spends on Earth, and its interaction with people and other angels.

The top triad, called Angels of Pure Contemplation, consists of seraphim, cherubim, and thrones. These high-ranking angels spend most of their time in communion with God. Seraphim are the highest of all, and their position is called First Hierarchy, First Choir. They are known as fiery serpents and appear with 6 wings, 4 heads, and fiery swords. They are beings of pure love, light, and fire, and prevent negative forces from attacking the divine. They shine so brilliantly with light that humans are unlikely to see them.

The middle triad, Angels of the Cosmos, is made up of angels called dominions, virtues, and powers. Dominions occupy the second hierarchy, first choir. Also known as lords, these angels are said to oversee other angels and interpret God's commands. Dominions also rule over earthly kingdoms and determine the outcome of wars. While performing their duties they have been seen in battle, in human form, riding red horses. They are also described as wearing crowns, golden robes and girdles, and green stoles. They have been depicted holding scepters and books.

The virtues are beneath the dominions and carry out their instructions. In this role, the virtues create miracles on Earth and help give power to humans to strengthen them for difficult tasks. Virtues are among 12 other angels who helped Eve prepare to give birth to Cain. They have been described as wearing garments of clergymen and carrying roses to symbolize Christ's passion.

## Guardian Angels

The lowest triad, Angels of the World, are called principalities, archangels, and angels. These spirits are said to live among people and are most likely to intervene in human affairs.

The principalities, or princedoms, are closest in appearance to people and watch over the visible human world. With princely powers they rule over the welfare of cities, states, and nations. In

the Old Testament these angels are referred to as the Prince of Persia and the Prince of Greece, both rulers with supernatural powers. They have been depicted wearing princely robes, golden belts, and crowns.

The lowest rank, simply known as angels, are defined in Psalms 91:11−13, which says God "has given his angels charge of you to guard you in all your ways. On their hands they will bear you up, lest you dash your foot against a stone." Angels can appear as soldiers, priests, or disguised as humans. They can carry many objects, including candles, scrolls, and shields.

## "I Love Her Before All Others"

While guardian angels are not specifically named in the Bible, the Hebrews believe that every person is assigned 11,000 of these spirits. In contrast, Christians are assigned only one guardian angel. There are exceptions to this idea, however. In the 1200s, Italian nun Umiltà of Faenza, or St. Humility, believed that she was watched over by 2 guardian angels. One of them, Emmanuel, was a fiery being of dazzling beauty with 6 wings. The other, Sapiel, or the Wisdom of God, was overwhelmingly beautiful and wore precious stones and garments of every color. St. Humility discussed many issues with her angels, from the majestic nature of God to the ordinary problems of founding a monastery. St. Humility describes her angels in her "Sermon of the Holy Angels" written around the beginning of the fourteenth century:

> I love all the angels of heaven, but two are the most
> cherished darlings of my joy who give me comfort
> day and night and offer me their gifts from the

bountiful wealth of their riches. My Lord assigned them to me as guardians so that they might protect me from all harm. . . . One comes from that order of angels who are given to Christians as guardians in this life. . . . Her appearance is of overwhelming beauty, like a precious stone or a pearl of great value. And I love her before all others that remain as her companions. She is called the angel Sapiel, a name that reason reveals as meaning divine wisdom. My heart fills with joy every time I hear the name. She has all the rich charms, all of which she bestows abundantly upon me. Indeed, having been present with me steadily from the moment I was born into this life, I know by her courtesy and courtly manners that she is full of piety. [6]

## Changing Images

St. Humility wrote about her beautiful guardian angel at the beginning of the Renaissance era. This period, which lasted roughly from the early fourteenth century to the mid-seventeenth century, was a time when great artists used angels as subjects in timeless works of art. Since most people were illiterate at that time, common ideas about how angels looked were shaped by these paintings and sculptures. In this way Renaissance painters, along with philosophers and religious scholars, helped reshape commonly held ideas about angels.

Before the Renaissance, angels were often depicted as towering male figures without wings. With their white robes, symbolic of heaven, clouds, and purity, they were beyond the reach of humans. However, Renaissance thinkers promoted the

*This statue of an angel is on top of a church in Europe. Angels are a common theme in architecture.*

idea that individuals could achieve a state of godliness similar to that of angels. This could be done by developing creativity and intellectual powers and by studying beauty and perfection. With this people-centered philosophy, lofty angels were shrunk down to human proportion during the Renaissance. Painters depicted the spirits wearing everyday clothes or dressed as soldiers in knight's armor often engaged in common tasks to emphasize their closeness to humanity.

# Wings, Women, and Babies

In the Bible the only angels with wings are seraphim. However, by the time of the Renaissance, wings were painted on nearly all angels. This has been traced to a renewed interest in Greek mythology and its many deities. The Greeks portrayed Nike, the goddess of victory, with two wings attached to the middle of her back. Discussing the symbolic meaning of wings in *Phaedrus,* Greek philosopher Plato wrote in 360 B.C.: "The wing is the corporeal [physical] element which is most akin to the divine, and which by nature tends to soar aloft and carry that which gravitates downwards into the upper region, which is the habitation of the gods. The divine is beauty, wisdom, goodness, and the like; and by these the wing of the soul is nourished, and grows apace."[7]

With a symbolic meaning steeped in beauty, wisdom, and goodness, it is not surprising Christian artists adopted classical Greek wings for their angel paintings. And the feathered appendages have several practical purposes beyond symbolism. They give angels a supernatural appearance while providing a way for them to fly around Earth and to and from heaven. And wings are an easy way for viewers to distinguish between angels and humans in paintings.

The gender of angels also began to change during the Renaissance. In the Bible all angels are male because early cultures did not associate women with powerful divine messengers. However, during the Renaissance, artists and philosophers promoted the idea that women were the ultimate form of divinely created beauty. Therefore, some angels in paintings took on clearly feminine traits.

Although angels in paintings of the Apocalypse remained muscular male warriors, scenes depicting the birth of Jesus often

# "Curiosity of the Human Mind"

Many modern concepts about angels were formed in the twelfth century. At that time religious scholars began analyzing spiritual beings in scientific terms developed by astronomers and biologists. This study led to a new field called angelology, later pursued by St. Thomas Aquinas and other theologians. In *Angels and Angelology in the Middle Ages* David Keck explores the development of this field:

> [The] early twelfth century witnessed people thinking about nature in new ways, probing the properties of human beings, plants, and rocks with scientific . . . interests. . . . Even in the field of [biblical miracles], instead of explaining the events by [attributing them] to the mi-

raculous intervention of God, people now explored the natural causes of events. . . . As the problems of nature became more pervasive in twelfth-century thought . . . so too would . . . the questions surrounding the nature of the angels. What was the natural condition of the angels? How were angels created? What kind of knowledge did they have? As Hugh of Saint Victor observes, the "curiosity of the human mind" is unable to rest from such questions. To investigate such problems was to inquire into the nature of the most sublime of God's creatures, to inquire into the height of God's creative act. By understanding the existence of the highest of creatures theologians explored the limits of the cosmos.

David Keck, *Angels and Angelology in the Middle Ages.* Oxford: Oxford University Press, 1998, p. 84.

feature angels with female faces, hair styles, and clothing. Even the archangel Gabriel is depicted as either a woman or androgynous, with both male and female features. Another reason for the feminizing of angels might be traced to the moral strictures of the day. It was simply more respectable for an androgynous or female angel to appear to Mary in her bedroom.

Another way to resolve gender issues in angels was traced to the Greek god Eros, known as Cupid by the Romans. As Nike's son, Eros was the god of lust and love. Often depicted as a young man with wings, Renaissance artists transformed Eros into an innocent child angel. This led to angels being portrayed as babies. Although cherubim are defined in the Bible as powerful creatures with four faces, both human and animal, child angels came to be called cherubs. Pudgy male baby angels were later called putti, the Italian word for boys. By the 1600s some cherubs had lost their bodies completely and were depicted simply as infant heads with wings.

However they are shown, Renaissance angels are some of the most beautiful beings ever painted on canvas. Artists portrayed them in idealized human form, dressed in exquisite gowns, with the glorious wings of eagles and swans. The works were painted in the striking colors of the rainbow because rainbows came to symbolize the angelic bridge between heaven and Earth.

The artist Raffaello Sanzio, or Raphael, was one of the most famous angel painters of the Renaissance. His 1515 work *Sistine Madonna* shows Mary standing on a cloud holding the infant Jesus. The clouds behind Mary depict the childlike faces of cherubic angels while two young angels, the same age as Jesus, are shown naked at the bottom of the picture. Their hair is windblown, and they each have a set of small, multicolored, birdlike wings.

Michelangelo, another renowned Renaissance artist, created the most famous pictures of angels on the ceiling of the Sistine Chapel. And the work influenced the way later artists depicted angels for centuries.

Michelangelo created nine elaborate paintings on the Sistine ceiling while lying on his back 68 feet (21m) above the floor. He covered the huge ceiling with 300 figures based on the book of Genesis. The paintings show dozens of angels in scenes from the creation of the universe, the Garden of Eden, and the story of Noah and the great flood. In one of the most dramatic scenes, the Last Judgment, angels are sounding trumpets to awaken the dead.

## Musical Angels

By the time Michelangelo finished the Sistine Chapel ceiling in 1480, musical angels had been around for about 100 years. They first appeared in illuminated manuscripts in Italy and France. These elaborately illustrated religious-themed books feature beautiful pictures of singing angels.

The concept of an angelic singer is derived from the Renaissance belief that divine messages delivered by winged spirits would be conveyed in perfect harmony. And by the early 1400s, the harmonious heralds were not only singing but playing harps, lutes, and even pipe organs. This followed the belief that the rich-sounding instruments with their divine harmony were symbolic of the cosmic power of God.

Hans Memling's 1490 *Christ Salvator Mundi Among Musical and Singing Angels* is perhaps the most elaborate painting of an angel band. Created on three large panels, the work features

"[God] has given his angels charge of you to guard you in all your ways. On their hands they will bear you up, lest you dash your foot against a stone."

—Psalms, describing the roles of guardian angels.

16 androgynous, winged, angel musicians and singers. Ancient stringed instruments include the psaltery, the harp, and the oddly named "angel's trumpet," a sticklike instrument with a string played with a bow. Newer instruments included the trombone and the portable organ.

## A Crown of Beauty

Angels are seen as not only projecting heavenly harmony but divine light as well. The Bible describes God as light and angels as fire, and radiant light has long been used to depict holiness. The ancient Egyptians painted rayed crowns around their gods, and the Greeks described their heroes as shining brighter than the sun. Around the fourth century, Christians began depicting an aura of light called a halo or nimbus hovering above the head of Jesus. By the 1300s, religious scholar William Durandus described all holy persons as wearing crowns of light, or halos: "The Just shall receive . . . a crown of beauty at the hands of the Lord, and a crown of this kind is shown in the form of a round shield, because they enjoy the divine protection."[8]

By the time Durandus wrote these words, angels and saints were commonly depicted with halos. Although halos fell out of fashion with painters by the middle Renaissance, people today continue to associate the glowing nimbus with angelic spirits.

## Angel Powers

Just as angel images have changed over the centuries, so too have the imagined powers of angels. While biblical angels are quite powerful, they most often appear as warriors and messengers. However, millions of people have claimed angelic visions and interventions over the years. Consequently, a wide array of

*Pope John Paul II baptizes an infant at the Sistine Chapel. The ceiling was painted by Michelangelo in the 1400s. The paintings show dozens of angels in scenes from the creation of the universe, the Garden of Eden, and the story of Noah and the great flood. In one of the scenes, the Last Judgment, angels sound trumpets to awaken the dead.*

supernatural powers that allow them to intercede in human affairs have been credited to angels. As Janice T. Connell writes in *Angel Power:*

> Angels see everything on earth, under the earth, in the depths of the seas, in the skies, and in the entire universe. They watch every event and listen to every word that is spoken, too. . . . The cosmic laws are managed by angels. Angels are quite capable of changing any of the cosmic laws in a split second. The power of angels is so great that any angel is capable of stopping a Comet in an instant. The angels derive their power from God, so nothing is beyond their strength. The earth, too, is managed by angels. Their job is to bring order out of chaos.[9]

With the ability to see everything and change cosmic laws, angels can allegedly control the weather. In the Bible, angelic visions are often accompanied by lightning, thunder, fire, and magnificent clouds. This has led to hundreds of stories that have been told of angels redirecting hurricanes and tornadoes and manipulating rain, wind, and snow. Control of earthquakes, which can cause massive deadly waves called tsunamis, are also within the realm of angel powers. According to theologian Timothy Snodgrass,

> Recently while traveling through Auckland, New Zealand, I was shown a vision of an angel descending into the bowels of the earth into key fault lines

*This engraving shows a group of angels praying. Around the fourth century, Christians began depicting an aura of light called a halo hovering above the head of Jesus. By the 1300s, most holy persons were depicted wearing crowns of light, or halos. People today continue to associate the glowing nimbus with angelic spirits.*

"Her appearance is of overwhelming beauty, like a precious stone or a pearl of great value. And I love her before all others that remain as her companions."

—St. Humility describing her guardian angel Sapiel.

and volcanic chambers in the South Pacific, working . . . to stabilize and minimize seismic events in this region. . . . [We] were shown that without angelic intervention, the South Pacific was due for a major seismic event which would produce tsunami in excess of 100 feet.[10]

## Healing Angels

Beyond cataclysmic events like earthquakes, angels are said to intercede in more personal ways. For example, they can use their supernatural powers to ease pain, heal wounds, cure disease, and save the dying. This may be done with direct intervention—the angel touches a sick or wounded person and miraculously heals him or her. This was said to have been the case for St. Simeon Stylites, who lived in the fifth century. In a search for divine knowledge, the saint spent the last 37 years of his life on top of a small platform located atop a 60-foot pillar (18m). St. Simeon survived because his followers hoisted food up to him using buckets and ropes.

The deprivation of living atop a pillar was not enough for the saint, so he ordered his disciples to tie him to the platform with rope. He was bound so tight that the rope cut into his flesh. However, it is documented that a guardian angel often visited the saint and healed his wounds by touching them.

In modern times, angelic healing sometimes takes a more creative approach. In *Where Miracles Happen* Joan Wester Anderson writes of Emily Weichman, a five-year-old who became deathly ill while on vacation with her parents in Yellowstone National Park. As Emily began to fade, her panicky parents drove for more than an hour to Rock Springs, Wyoming. But when they arrived in town they had no idea where the hospital was located. They were soon relieved to see an oddly lit, large blue sign pointing toward a hospital. Then they saw another and another. The signs guided the Weichmans to the hospital until Emily could safely be taken into the emergency room. As a doctor stabilized her condition, Emily's mother told him she was grateful for the hospital signs. The doctor replied "What signs? . . . I live about eight miles out on that road. I travel it every day. . . . I've never seen any hospital

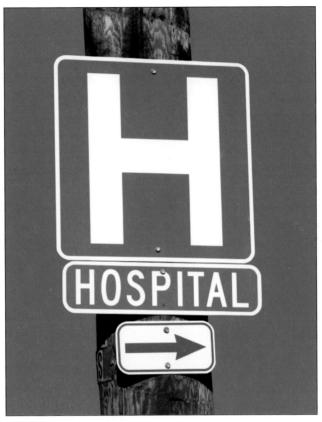

*This common sign directs people to the closest hospital. While on vacation, a family reported seeing these signs when their daughter became ill, but locals claim no such signs exist in the area. The family came to believe the signs were sent by angels to guide them in their time of need.*

signs."[11] Later, after Emily was released, her family drove around for more than an hour looking for the hospital signs. They finally concluded that an angel had provided divine directions to save their daughter's life.

## Mysterious Strangers

Angels can help others by assuming human form. These angels are referred to as mysterious strangers because they appear suddenly, provide aid, and disappear in an instant.

Mysterious strangers can be men, women, or children, and be of any race. In most descriptions, however, they are well-dressed, attractive, clean-cut, and young. However, people who have encountered mysterious strangers sometimes describe features that distinguish the angel from an average person. For example, in *Angels over Their Shoulders* an observer named Eugene Martin describes the unearthly appearance of an angel that helped him: "Its garments were celestial green, and a soft golden aura enveloped the length of its form."[12]

Whatever they look like, mysterious strangers are said to speak firmly and politely, but sparingly. They often have inexplicable knowledge of the crisis at hand and are able to calmly, yet forcefully, guide events in a positive direction.

The archangel Raphael is a biblical example of the mysterious stranger. He appeared suddenly in the guise of a man to guide Tobit on a journey. In modern times the deeds of mysterious strangers have filled dozens of best-selling books about angels. The visitor who aided the Reverend Maurice Coers at the Immanuel Baptist Church in Covington, Kentucky, is typical of the mysterious stranger.

The church was built on a scenic towering bluff above the Ohio River. During the winter of 1958, however, the hillside began to collapse, and the church started to slide down toward the river. Efforts were made to shore up the hill, but engineers felt the site was unsafe and the church would have to be abandoned. Coers was heartbroken and began making plans to relocate. However, several months later a large man wearing bib overalls and weighing at least 300 pounds (136kg) unexpectedly appeared at the church site. He approached Coers and said that he knew about the landslide under the church. Coers showed him the slipping dirt and mud along the hill. The man said he was an engineer who built railroads through the Rocky Mountains. He drew up plans for a retaining wall similar to the type used in railroad construction and then disappeared as suddenly as he had arrived. The wall was built, and the church remains standing today. As Anderson writes in *Where Angels Walk:*

> Few visitors . . . notice the retaining wall, although an occasional engineer marvels at its unique structure and design. But no one can explain who was responsible for it. For the considerate contractor never submitted a bill to the church board. Nor was he a member of any engineering fraternity, or listed among the certified engineers in the United States or, despite his imposing appearance, ever seen in the area again. But . . . the wall speaks silently but powerfully of things unseen.[13]

## Many Blessed Armies

The powers and appearances of angels have changed considerably over the centuries. Once they appeared as astonishing heavenly warriors with flaming swords. Now they may be seen as engineers in overalls or winged babies playing harps. But this change can be traced back hundreds of years to early theologians such as Dionysius, who wrote in the fifth century, "There are many blessed armies of the heavenly intelligences, surpassing the weak and

*Sixteenth-century French Protestant theologian John Calvin believed that angels helped people on an everyday basis by guiding them in the right direction and by trying to ward off evil influences.*

limited reckoning of our material numbers."[14]

It is little wonder that believers see angels in thousands of different guises performing an infinite variety of tasks. Whether these angels are from the highest or lowest hierarchy, their powers far surpass those of humans. But angels have also become humanized, appearing in mundane forms that people can easily relate to. Believers say this is all part of the Creator's plan to touch lives and guide the intricate machinery of the universe.

Without angels, people would be at the mercy of random events with no divine assistance. In the sixteenth century, French Protestant theologian John Calvin described the contributions the spirits make to humanity: "The angels are the dispensers and administrators of the divine [generosity] toward us; they regard our safety, undertake our defense, direct our ways, and exercise a constant [concern] that no evil befall us."[15]

# CHAPTER 3

# Angel Encounters

The story has been told countless times over the years. Someone is in immediate danger—threatened by a wild animal, or in a car that breaks down in a storm, or is very sick and far from a hospital. In a moment of despair the victim prays, and a form of rescue presents itself. A guide arrives on horseback, a tow truck driver stops, a voice on the radio offers directions. When the victim is brought to safety and turns to offer thanks, the rescuer is gone, leaving no footprints, tire tracks, or any other evidence of his or her existence. The rescued individual searches for days but can find no record of the rescuer. The saved person comes to believe that angelic interference occurred in his or her life. It is a tale as old as humanity and as recent as the latest angel blog on the Internet.

But angels do not only rescue people in immediate danger. They are also said to cure cancer and other fatal diseases, lift people out of depression, and offer guidance in economic affairs. People have also reported angels helping them with less essential tasks. An anonymous contributor to the Encounters with Angels Web site claims that her parents were very poor. Her situation was so desperate she had no nice clothes to wear to her first day of junior high. The girl was feeling sad and prayed for new clothes. Moments later she looked out the window and saw a woman pull up to the house in a nice new car. The woman talked to the girl's mother, handed her something, and left. The girl believes the lady was guided to her by an angel:

> [She] had a bag of clothes. She told my mother she had bought them for her daughter, but her daughter didn't like them. She was going to throw the dresses away, but had an overpowering urge to bring them to our house. We never saw that lady again. In the bag were five dresses. They still had the price tags on them. I am very short; I have to hem everything. Those dresses were my size and the right color for my complexion. Most surprising, I didn't have to hem them.[16]

Many who report such stories prefer to remain anonymous. Average people who experience supernatural phenomena are afraid of receiving unwanted attention. Some have lost jobs and had their sanity called into question when they have reported angelic encounters. However, people in all walks of life say they have been touched by an angel.

During the American Revolution General George Washington and his men were stationed at Valley Forge, Pennsylvania. Washington reported that he was offered advice by a guardian angel while his troops were freezing outside.

During the American Revolution, it is said, George Washington was offered advice by a guardian angel while his troops were freezing at Valley Forge. Even atheists, or those who do not believe in God, have claimed angel encounters. In 1985 6 cosmonauts aboard a Soviet space station orbiting Earth said they were visited by angels. These men were not religious but stated that, after 155 days in outer space, they were blinded by a bright orange light outside their windows. After their eyes adjusted to the radiant brilliance, they saw 7 giant angels floating through space. The beings had human form but had wings and misty halos. They appeared to be hundreds of feet tall and had the wingspans of huge jetliners.

## When Angels Appear

Reports of awe-inspiring angels in outer space are dramatic and newsworthy. But the experience of the Soviet cosmonauts fits an age-old pattern of angel encounters. From the Bible story of Ezekiel to modern sightings, many angel visits begin when the heavens open up to reveal a dazzling light. This is followed by the advent of angels. In *Touched by Angels* Eileen Elias Freeman describes various reports of heavenly illumination. Observers have described this light as "white, brighter than any white I've ever seen," "iridescent, like mother-of-pearl," "colors I've never seen on earth," "if a diamond were made of silver," and "if sunlight were blue and full of glitter."[17]

Angels have also been reported traveling down glimmering shafts of light from the sky. Others have been seen materializing out of a cloud that draws near the observer. Sometimes an angel is simply seen walking at a distance but suddenly appears very close.

Like ghosts, angels are often reported walking through walls or closed doors to enter or exit a room. At other times, footsteps are heard, and the spirit knocks on the door. When the percipient opens the door the angel is revealed.

Some encounters with angels begin when a mysterious cloud suddenly appears in a closed room, revealing an angel. Angels are also said to become visible on a wall like a picture. An observer named Tasha describes one such angelic vision she had as a small child growing up in a troubled home:

> I remember sitting directly in front of a wall, and I couldn't take my eyes off of the wall. I felt like I was being pulled into place and held in front of the wall. I had been staring at it awhile when I saw a figure in the wall. I was seeing a man's face, shoulders and wings in the background. Every part of him I was seeing had a light bluish tint to it. He had a very pretty face, like he was in his 20s. His eyes were a darker shade of blue than the rest of him, and he had medium-long hair flowing around him. . . . He was smiling and giggling with me as I smiled and giggled back. He had the most gorgeous wings, and when he giggled his wings fluttered up and down. I couldn't talk much or understand many words, but he "told" me—like he sent a message directly into my mind—that everything would be okay.[18]

Although Tasha's angel appeared on the wall and looked human, except for his blue tint, angels can appear in many other guises.

During the American Revolution George Washington was purportedly offered advice from a guardian angel while his troops were freezing at Valley Forge.

For example recipients have reported stone statues of angels coming to life to offer aid. Angels have also emerged from pictures and paintings. People have even claimed that their pet dog, cat, or bird turned out to be a guardian angel.

On rare occasions more than one person can see an angel. In these situations, however, each individual might perceive the angel in a different way. One person will report seeing a ball of light, another a floating cloud in the room, yet another will see a human form with wings. Another person in the room might see nothing at all or hear only a disembodied voice.

And it seems angels have adopted to modern technology. Angel voices are heard on telephones and digital recorders, their faces reportedly appear on televisions, and people with cameras and video recorders have photographed them.

## Night Visits

Many angelic encounters are dismissed as dreams because they happen late at night while the observer is in bed. Typically, the percipient is awakened by a visitor bending over his or her body or standing by the foot of the bed. After such visitations, the observer might have a prophetic vision and see into the future. It is not unusual for a person in such a situation to report receiving a miraculous cure or an unlikely solution to a perplexing problem.

People who have angelic night visions sometimes report being taken on out-of-body experiences through time and space. In such cases, the recipient's body is seen lying in bed as he or she flies through the ceiling holding an angel's hand. The angel might take the individual to a destination hundreds of miles from home in an instant. The traveler may see loved ones in danger or lying sick in a hospital bed. On more prophetic journeys, travelers can be taken to visit events that happened in the past or will come to pass in the future. They may even visit hell to learn what awaits them if they do not change their wicked ways.

The concept of traveling though time and space is not limited to angel sightings. Countless people tell similar tales about ghosts or space aliens in UFOs. However, these people frequently say they were extremely frightened by the event. Some never get over the feelings of fear generated by the meeting. But those who encounter angels most often report feeling calm, happy, and relieved. Some have said that these positive feelings remain with them every day.

## Dramatic Rescues

Many purported angel encounters are experienced by innocent and vulnerable children. One remarkable rescue was reported in *Angels over Their Shoulders* by angel investigators Brad Steiger and Sherry Hansen Steiger. The story was told by Myrna Martinson whose nine-year-old daughter Tammy was staying with her grandparents. Myrna said she was awakened from a deep sleep by an otherworldly spirit that told her to pray for one hour. After doing so she fell back into a blissful sleep. Several hours later the telephone rang. It was a fireman who told Martinson that Tammy had been trapped in a bedroom in her grandparent's burning house. The fireman said the room was completely engulfed in flames when he entered, but Tammy was safe in the corner, protected by an awesome silver and white being that stood over her and kept the flames at bay. When asked about the timing of the event, Martinson learned that the angel saved her child while she had been praying. After Tammy returned home, she confirmed the appearance of the silver and white guardian angel protecting her that night from the fire.

*This angel, with a sickle and stalks of grain, represents death. Many people who have had near-death experiences report angels guiding and comforting them in their time of confusion. These angels of death don't necessarily mean the person will die, as they reportedly seem to answer questions and calm confusion.*

Oftentimes, those who meet their guardian angels can depend on them for help and advice their entire lives. This was the case for Diana Osornio, a 50-year-old psychologist from Minnesota. Osornio first encountered her guardian angel when she was five years old and vacationing in the woods with her parents. According to Osornio, "I was shown bits and pieces of my future life. . . . My angel told me that I had a distinct purpose in life and a particular mission to accomplish. Of course, much of what he said went over my head at the time. Throughout my life I have continually flashed back to that initial visit and remembered more of what the angel told me."[19]

When Osornio was 11, her guardian returned to save her life when she was once again on vacation. She had been swimming in a lake and got trapped under the planks of a wooden pier. She was unconscious and about to die when witnesses said "a guy who kind of looked like a hippie, with long blond hair,"[20] pulled her from the water and saved her. Her parents searched every cabin at the resort to find the man to thank him, but he could not be found. No one had ever seen the stranger, but Osornio believes it was her guardian angel.

Ever since her rescue, Osornio says she has had mental imagery that has helped save her from sickness or injury. She has heard a voice in her head telling her to avoid a specific road where a traffic accident would occur. She has even had premonitions to take certain healing herbs in a specific sequence. Although she knew nothing about the herbs, she says: "Research after the fact . . . [showed] that this formula was what I needed at the time for a major [healing] of my physical body."[21] Although Osornio never saw an angel, she has seen bright white light that she believes is a manifestation of her guardian spirit.

## Angels and Adolescents

Adolescence is a tough time for many, and it seems guardian angels often appear to rescue troubled teens. Sometimes angels provide money to fund a life-changing event. This happened to 14-year-old Sharon Olson who says in *Angels over Their Shoulders* that an angel with silky, feathery wings left a pile of money on her kitchen table so she could attend music camp. She met a teacher there who played a crucial role in her musical development. Olsen is now a respected musician who teaches and performs inspirational music.

Teens who have suffered emotional and physical abuse have been saved by angels in their darkest moments. A girl named Jane told one such story on the Paranormal Phenomena Web site. She said her first boyfriend died when she was in seventh grade. Two years later she was sexually assaulted by a person she thought was her friend. Jane was so depressed she considered suicide. Unexpectedly, a friend she had not seen since second grade called her when her mood was at its lowest ebb. He told her life would get better and offered to visit and talk. Jane and her friend grew very close, and he promised her that he would be by her side forever. Jane says they learned to read each other's thoughts without speaking. She finally asked him if he was her guardian angel, and he answered yes. Jane says the angel has been giving her advice since that time.

## Escorts to the Other Side

Jane's angel came to her at a crucial time when she was about to take her own life. This seems to be a typical trait of angels. They arrive when people are about to cross the threshold from life to death. Oftentimes this is said to happen when a person has

*This angel, depicted in an old woodcut, appeared to a family in Israel that was having financial problems. Angels have appeared to people who have had all types of problems.*

been in a serious accident or is very sick and about to die. These people experience near-death experiences, or NDEs. During their time at death's door, they report angelic encounters before being brought back to life.

Many stories about NDEs share many similar traits. Victims

# Angel Pets

A ngels do not appear as animals in the Bible. However, in recent years many occurrences have been reported of deceased pets returning to their owners as angels. In *Answers from the Angels* by Terry Lynn Taylor, Linda Kramer tells the story of Benjie, a dog she bought as a puppy. Benjie lived with Kramer for 16 years as she suffered through thyroid cancer, a traumatic divorce, and a debilitating battle with rheumatoid arthritis. After Benjie's death Kramer says she made contact with his angelic spirit while practicing transcendental meditation:

have out-of-body experiences and float above their dying bodies. They have soaring sensations as if flying and experience feelings of confusion. Some move down a tunnel toward a very bright light. During this time they are often accompanied by angel guides as they walk toward the light. Feelings of bewilderment are replaced by sensations of calm and acceptance as the angel

> I entered into a large open area filled with hosts of angels. The sweet smells, soft colors, and intense feelings of peace and joy were embodied in what seemed like hundreds of angels in traditional form. Suddenly, across the open space . . . Benjie came running toward me. He jumped into my arms and tried to lick my face . . . when suddenly I was embraced by a beautiful androgynous angel. The implication was clear to me: Benjie had been an angel all the time. . . . I felt humbled that such a great being as an angel would have spent sixteen earthbound years as my companion.

Terry Lynn Taylor, *Answers from the Angels.* Tiburon, CA: HJ Kramer, 1993, p. 142.

guides introduce the victims to dead relatives and friends who are also in the company of angels. At this time, their lives pass before their eyes, and they clearly see happy and sad experiences from their pasts. After reviewing their lives, observers may hear celestial music and see extremely moving visions of paradise. However, the moment they are about to enter heaven, the angel

Guardian angels
are often said to
appear to rescue
troubled teens.

tells them they are not ready yet. Reluctantly, the souls fly back to Earth and reenter their broken bodies. Although few wish to return to Earth after seeing heaven, most who go through NDEs are able to heal with remarkable speed and are positively affected by their angelic journey the rest of their lives.

The brush with death that David Goines describes on the Child's Near Death Experiences Web site contains nearly every element of a typical NDE. Goines was 13 when he was struck by a cement mixer while riding his bicycle to school. He remembers the initial panic as he saw the massive truck bearing down on him. But he recalls nothing else until he felt himself floating above a scene in an emergency room. As he looked down, Goines saw half a dozen doctors and nurses working over his body, which was completely entangled in his bike frame. He saw a welder arrive to remove the frame from the mangled body. Unable to watch the gruesome scene, Goines turned to run away and found himself in total darkness as if in a lightless tunnel. Goines took another step and was instantly transported to the most beautiful garden he had ever seen. According to Goines:

> This garden was like a formal terrace which had been carved out of a rough mountain, just a few feet below the peak. Everything was white marble and evergreen. The air was so incredibly light and clear and fresh and cool. It seemed like I was breathing pure chilled oxygen. The garden was trimmed in evergreen shrubs, each a perfect specimen; and the fragrance of evergreen lightly scented the air. This place seemed so perfect in every detail. Directly in front of me, just a few steps away, was a

marble bench which seemed to invite me to come, sit, and rest. As I sat down and breathed in the fresh wonderful air, I looked around. . . . The floor was flat and smooth, polished to perfection such that it looked seamless. This garden terrace was surrounded by low marble pillars and a marble railing and looked like it had been formed right out of the side of the mountain in one seamless effort.[22]

While taking in the scene, Goines saw a kindly old gentleman materialize on the bench next to him. The angel's blue eyes sparkled as he told Goines that he was not dead but that his body was in a lot of trouble. However, the angel assured Goines he was safe and would fully recuperate. The young man and the angel communicated telepathically as Goines asked many questions. In explaining the situation, the angel told him: "It is your mental and spiritual body that is here. It is with your mental and spiritual eyes that you see this place. . . . This place is in your mind's eye, your imagination. . . . I am here for you on behalf of your heavenly Father's love for you and to remind you from where you came." [23] As soon as Goines's mind was able to grasp this information, the angel disappeared. The young man arose and climbed the nearby mountain which he said was filled with astoundingly beautiful flowers, lush grasses, and crystal clear rivers. However, he had a realization that he was not yet ready to remain in paradise.

Goines ran back down the mountain path, stumbling and falling as he returned to the marble bench. Suddenly he awoke in the hospital. His broken body was in massive pain and immobilized in 5-way traction. Goines was told he had been in a coma for 21 days.

His experience in the garden had taken place over the course of 3 weeks. Although he required physical therapy for a year after his accident, Goines was able to persevere thanks to the angelic vision he received during his near-death experience.

## The Angels of Mons

The story told by Goines cannot be backed up by other witnesses. However, in some very unusual circumstances, the appearance of angels can be verified by more than one person. And one of the most famous angelic group encounters took place during the first battle of World War I.

On August 23, 1914, a small company of British soldiers clashed with a much larger German contingent near Mons, Belgium. Despite being vastly outnumbered, the British were able to repel the highly trained Germans. This victory gave the British public hope that the war would be short and easy. Within a few months, however, the war had grown into a massive bloodbath as tens of thousands of soldiers on both sides were killed.

In April 1915, when British morale was at a low ebb, a story appeared in the *Spiritualist* magazine about the Battle of Mons. The story claimed that a supernatural force appeared to help the British miraculously hold off the Germans in this initial battle.

After the story was published, several officers who said they fought at the Battle of Mons affirm the tale of divine intervention. It was said to begin with the prayers of a soldier in the trenches. This man invoked the spirit of fourth-century Roman soldier St. George, patron saint of England, who called forth angelic warriors. These heavenly bowmen appeared as British knights dressed in armor like those who fought in France at the Battle of Agincourt in 1415. Although they were armed only with bows and arrows,

*This wood-cut shows a woman deep in thought receiving a message from a messenger angel. Messenger angels are similar to guardian angels, appearing to people when they most need help.*

"I was shown bits and pieces of my future life. . . . My angel told me that I had a distinct purpose in life and a particular mission to accomplish."

—Psychologist Diana Osornio explaining the role played by her guardian angel.

the angelic knights helped drive the Germans from Mons.

The story about the angels at Mons was used by British politicians and priests to claim that God was on their side in World War I. Drawings of the angels of Mons appeared in the press, and songs were written about the event. The story was also picked up by the world media. The stories reaffirmed as undeniable proof that divine providence was on the side of the British and their allies, including the United States.

As the story continued, it was embellished. It was said that fifteenth-century saint Joan of Arc appeared over the battlefield. Another soldier said the angels were cavalrymen, not knights. Whatever the case, in the years after the war the angels of Mons story remained popular but was never conclusively proved. Some say the soldiers were suffering from extreme fatigue and were hallucinating when they saw the angels. Believers maintain the victory was due to angelic interference. As with most other stories of angelic interference, the dispute cannot be resolved.

## New Age Angels

Throughout history most people who encountered angels, whether they were soldiers, mothers, or children, were deeply religious. However, in recent years a new type of angelic encounter with less religious overtones has occurred. Believers in New Age spiritualism are generally less involved with organized religion. Some are part of the nature-based Wiccan religion, sometimes called pagan, magick, or witchcraft. Whatever their beliefs, they often use magical rituals and their own personal powers to summon angels into their lives. They do so because they believe that angels can act as spirit guides to provide them with happiness, romance, and wealth. Commenting on this branch of angelology,

Wiccan author and high priestess Silver Raven Wolf writes in *Angels: Companions in Magick:*

> I have found that angels appear to transcend all cultures, races, and systems. They are a part of human history and civilization, sometimes at the forefront, other times in the shadows, but they are always there. They don't belong to any one particular religion although many modern people try to associate them with Christianity, Judaism, and Islam. No one religion holds total responsibility for the belief in angels. In truth, these religions only support the existence of angels, they didn't create them. . . . [However,] I have discovered . . . angels aren't anybody's property. Angels don't belong to any particular religious system. Angels create bridges between various religions. To call on an angel is to rise above religious dogma and touch the universal spirit.[24]

New Age concepts are based on ancient indigenous teachings that say spirits exist in every aspect of nature, including rocks, trees, clouds, and planets in the sky. With spirits everywhere in nature, it is not surprising that believers would encounter angels while walking in a forest. This was the case with Sylvia, who described her experience to Silver Raven Wolf. Sylvia went camping in a wild Montana forest in the Rocky Mountains to seek out angel guides. As night was falling on the primitive woodland, Sylvia conducted a ritual on an improvised altar laid out with incense, candles, and precious stones. After chanting

some homemade poetry to invoke an angelic appearance, Sylvia crawled into her tent and fell asleep.

Hours later, Sylvia was awakened when her nearly dead campfire flared brightly, nearly touching the lower branches of a tall pine tree. Sylvia sat up abruptly, peered into the fire, and saw an unusual figure.

> At first I didn't realize she was my guardian angel. She was a Native American maiden with long, black braids. I loved the impish grin on her face. She didn't have wings but could fly anyway. Her dress was brown with a colorful, beaded design of red, yellow, and black. She told me she'd been with me since the day I was born. . . . She said she can heal, and she said she would be with me until the day I die.[25]

Since Sylvia first met her guardian angel, she says she has received help and guidance in several important aspects of her life. The angel advised Sylvia in her musical career, on matters of love, and in decisions concerning financial affairs.

## Changed Lives

Sylvia met her angel under different circumstances than most. However, her New Age invocations, candles, and incense could be compared with those used in traditional religious ceremonies. Whatever the situation, hers is just one of thousands of angel visitations reported every year.

In order to learn more about these visits Brad Steiger and Sherry Hansen Steiger conducted a survey of 20,000 people who said they had angelic encounters. The investigators found that 90 percent of the respondents had their first angelic encounters around the age of 5, and most had crystal clear memories of the incidents despite their young age. Of the respondents to the survey, 50 percent said they were convinced their guardian angel watched over them at all times. An equal number said angels at one time or another healed them physically or mentally.

A large number of respondents reported supernatural abilities they credit to angelic interference. Ninety percent said they had telepathic experiences; that is, they were able to communicate mentally with another person without speaking. About 75 percent reported out-of-body experiences, and half claimed they were clairvoyant—they could see into the future or distant past. The clairvoyance led to prophetic dreams or visions of events that later came true.

These numbers show that countless people believe their daily lives have been touched by angels. While scientific evidence does not back the existence of divine beings, a person's spiritual experiences are difficult to deny. And most who have had angelic encounters are adamant in their belief that the incident was genuine. Their lives were changed by angels, and their faith in divine guidance is all the proof they need.

# CHAPTER 4

# Fallen Angels

In the Bible the devil is referred to by 33 different names, including Satan, Lucifer, Beelzebub, the Old Serpent, the Enemy, and the Ruler of Darkness. He is blamed for a host of sins, evils, and human misery. But Satan is also unquestionably an angel. In the book of Revelation, he is the angel of the bottomless pit. In Corinthians he is transformed into an angel of light. In Isaiah he is the angel of the morning that has fallen from heaven. But Satan is not the only fallen angel.

At one time all angels were good. But those who displeased God were punished by banishment from heaven. In the book of Enoch, hundreds of fallen angels are identified as ones who left heaven to corrupt humanity.

The book of Enoch defines four grades of fallen angels. The first is Satanail, or Satan, the prince of the fallen angels who thought he was greater than God. For this sin he was cast from heaven on the second day of creation. Describing this event in *The Secret*

*This English woodcut shows a version of the Devil. He is grotesquely formed and frightens everyone who sees him.*

*History of Lucifer,* author Lynn Picknett writes: "[God] was confronted by one of his own leading angels, Lucifer, in a sort of explosive palace coup—which of course, failed spectacularly, ending with the rebel leader's banishment to Earth, and beyond, into the nightmarish realms of hell."[26]

Other angels who were evicted from heaven include 200 watchers. These were children of heaven that decided to mate with the beautiful women of Earth. After doing so, they fathered a race of giants called Nephilim that ate human flesh and drank blood. In addition to their sinful couplings, various watchers are responsible for teaching humans to make weapons of war and for instructing them in the practice of magic, astrology, and alchemy.

Another type of angel is called an apostate. These are followers of Satan who plotted against God with him. Unlike other fallen angels, apostates regret their rebellion and are said to weep uncontrollably and repeatedly ask Enoch to pray for them. A final grade of fallen angel is simply called an angel. These are Satan's helpers who are said to be imprisoned under the earth in hell.

## Souls Underground

The idea of spirits living beneath the earth is as old as humanity. Around 5000 B.C. the ancient Sumerians wrote about an underground land of the dead. Their concepts of this land are strikingly similar to images of hell in the Bible. It was filled with boats and boatmen, impassible mountains, gates and guardians, and other barriers to free movement. In later centuries the Greeks described a place called Hades where unhappy souls dwelt while endlessly wishing for a return to their lives aboveground.

The Zoroastrians, whose beliefs later influenced Judeo-Christian angelology, say a fallen spirit lives under the earth. This angel, the Lord of the Lies, sends his devils forth from their underground lair to torment humanity.

Christians also believe that the fiery pits of hell were created for Satan and other fallen angels. Moreover, hell is a place where nonbelievers, escorted by angels, go after death. As Matthew 13:41–42 states: "[Jesus] will send his angels and they will gather out of his kingdom all the causes of sin and all evildoers, and throw them into the furnace of fire; there men will weep and gnash their teeth."

Since millions of souls are said to wind up in hell, fallen angels are necessary to run this place filled with foul smells, smoke, misery, and torment. In hell the body is supposedly attacked by wild beasts and eaten by huge, fire-breathing worms. Sinners are hung by their eyelashes. And the angels of punishment oversee such heinous tortures, acting as emissaries of Satan.

## Life in Hell

The fallen angels of hell are said to exist in a hierarchy as complex as that of the angels in heaven. This hierarchy is outlined in an early who's who of hell, *Fortress of the Faith*, published in 1467 by Spanish monk Alphonsus de Spina. An expert in demonology, or the study of demons, de Spina concluded that there are 10 orders

**"QUOTE"**

"[God] was confronted by one of his own leading angels, Lucifer, in a sort of explosive palace coup—which of course, failed spectacularly, ending with the rebel leader's banishment . . . into the nightmarish realms of hell."

—Author Lynn Picknett describing how Lucifer came to be the ruler of hell.

of demons that include millions of fallen angels. These angels fit into nine specific categories: false gods, inquisitors, creators of tempests, tempters, accusers, deluders, furies, vengeful spirits, and lying spirits. Within those ranks demons include angels who are in disguise, those who assail saints, and those who persuade humans to sin.

Another source of demonology, *Dictionnaire Infernal,* written by French occultist Collin de Plancy in 1818, includes the names and description of many fallen angels and their hierarchies. Some of these demons spend all their time on earth, some travel between earth and hell, and some stay exclusively in hell.

The chief of the fallen angels is Semyaza. He is the leader of the watchers who encourages other angels to mate with mortals. It is said that he now hangs between Earth and heaven and may be seen in the constellation Orion. Semyaza has 2 sons, Hiwa and Hiya, who were born of Eve's daughter. These half-human, half-fallen-angel creatures are so hungry they eat 1,000 camels, 1,000 horses, and 1,000 oxen every day.

Other demons who stay in the underworld work in various aspects to torment sinners, spread evil, and keep hell functioning. The hated demon Xaphan, or Zephon, is an apostate angel who rebelled with Satan. He tried to set heaven on fire before the fallen angels could be cast out. As punishment, he is forced to use his hands and mouth to stoke the fires of hell for eternity.

## Dukes, Patrons, and Punishers

According to demonologists, hell is strikingly similar to the royalty of medieval society, said to be filled with nobility and military commanders. For example, Alocer is a grand duke of hell who commands 36 legion of devils. (In ancient Rome, a legion was an army division that consisted of 3,000 to 6,000 soldiers.) Astroth is named by de Plancy as the grand duke of western hell. Once he was an angel prince in the order of thrones, but now he appears either as a foul angel or a beautiful angel riding a dragon and carrying a viper in his right hand. Whatever his guise, Astroth's breath stinks so bad that the evil odor cannot be defended against. Astroth commands 40 legions of devils and encourages people to be lazy and useless. Like several other fallen angels, Astroth believes he was unjustly punished by God and will someday return to his rightful place in heaven.

Adramelech, or the "king of fire" is the high chancellor of hell and president of the High Council of Devils. A fallen angel beaten in combat by archangels Uriel and Raphael, it is said that Adramelech is as evil as Satan. According to *The Messiah* by nineteenth-century German poet Friedrich Gottlieb Klopstock, Adramelech is "the enemy of God, greater in malice, guile, ambition, and mischief than Satan, a fiend more curst, a deeper hypocrite."[27] It is said that the people of a city of the ancient Assyrians, Sepharvaim, sacrificed children to him.

In addition to hell's royalty, several fallen angels oversee various professions in the manner of evil patron saints. For example, Kobal is called the patron of comedians and the director of hellish entertainments. Murmur is the demon of musicians that manifests himself as a warrior astride a gryphon, a monster with the head and wings of an eagle and the body and tail of a lion. Nybbas is publicist of the pleasures of hell who manages visions and dreams. He is regarded as a buffoon and a charlatan who can entice mortals into hell by promising unearthly gratifications.

Various sins and disagreeable habits also have their own devils. Verin is the demon of impatience, and Succorbenoth is the demon of jealousy. Sonneillon, a fallen angel from the throne triad, is the demon of hate that gained great fame in the seventeenth century.

Sonneillon was said to possess the body of a French nun in 1616. When she was only 16, Sister Madeleine de la Palud began to exhibit signs of possession. Her body became hideously contorted, and she angrily destroyed a crucifix as other nuns watched in horror. This blasphemy occurred during the height of French witch hysteria when thousands of women were falsely accused of consorting with the devil. Under torture Sister Madeleine signed a confession saying that Sonneillon had indeed taken control of her soul: "With all my heart and . . . with all my will most deliberately do I wholly renounce God, Father, Son, and Holy Ghost . . . all the Angels and especially my guardian angel . . . [and] my lot in Paradise."[28]

## Hell's Bureaucrats

Other fallen angels of hell are said to work in the underworld bureaucracy. Melchom is the treasurer of hell, cast down to the underworld after Hebrew king David took his holy crown. His crime was wanting to own all of creation. As a lesser demon of hell, Melchom is known as the paymaster of hell's servants and the one who carries the purse. His other job is appearing aboveground to instill greed in humans. In this guise he appears either as a fat merchant, a handsome soldier, or even Santa Claus. Since war is good for the greedy, Melchom is known to incite bloody conflicts and then reap profits from the misery.

According to de Plancy, Nergal is the chief of hell's secret police and an honorary spy in the service of Beelzebub. He is depicted with a lion's head, wings, and clawed feet. He is also regarded as the angel of war, pestilence, and fever.

## The Princes of Hell

Some of hell's angels work closer to Satan than others. These great princes of hell are fallen archangels that help Satan commit his foul tasks and oversee his wicked kingdom. Although some of their names have become synonymous with Satan, historically, they are individual fallen angels with their own characteristics.

Of the most fearsome of dark princes, Azazel is the lord of hell and the seducer of humankind. In his true form he is a demon with 7 serpent heads, 14 faces, and 12 wings. He was cast from heaven for failing to bow down to Adam when the first human was presented to God and the assembled angels of heaven. For this refusal he was henceforth called Satan's standard bearer. Enoch 8:1–3 describes a few of Azazel's many evil deeds, which include teaching men to make weapons and women to use cosmetics:

> Azazel taught men to make swords and knives and shields and breastplates; and made known to them the metals [of the earth] and the art of working them; and [he taught women to make] bracelets and ornaments; and the . . . beautifying of the eyelids; and all kinds of costly stones and all coloring tinctures. And there arose much godlessness, and they committed fornication, and they were led astray and became corrupt in all their ways.

Mephistopheles is another powerful prince of hell closely associated with Satan. But while Satan appears with cloven hooves, horns, and a tail, Mephistopheles, whose name in Hebrew means "he who loves not the light," resembles a human. This demon is often pictured as a tall man dressed in black from head to toe. Mephistopheles recruits mortals to sell their souls to Satan in exchange for money, love, power, and talent. The demon carries a red book for the sinners to sign for this purpose.

Those who sign the red book of Mephistopheles have their signatures notarized by Baal, hell's master of rituals and pacts. This demon was once the high god of Canaan and lord of life. But he engaged in a battle with death and was sent to the underworld. There he rules 66 legions of devils. Baal appears with 3 heads, that of a toad, a man, and a cat. Black magicians who wish to become invisible invoke his name.

Whatever the powers of Baal and Mephistopheles, Beelzebub is the prince of all princes, said to have powers only second to Satan's. In heaven he was the highest-ranking angel. Since his fall, Beelzebub is the chief of demons who resembles a giant fly, hence his nickname, "Lord of the Flies." Also known as the "Lord of Chaos," Beelzebub explains his mission to Hebrew king Solomon in the Book of Solomon 6:1–4: "I bring destruction by means of tyrants; I cause the demons to be worshiped alongside men; and I arouse desire in holy men and select priests. I bring about jealousies and murders in a country, and I instigate wars."

## The Leader of the Pack

While many atrocities are said to be committed by the princes of hell, most are blamed on Satan. Christians say Satan is the embodiment of all evil and the tempter of humanity. Those who give in to his nefarious ways are condemned to everlasting hell.

Since the Middle Ages, Satan has been portrayed in a manner similar to Pan, the Greek god of nature. Pan is said to have a human head and torso with the hind legs, ears, and horns of a goat. This image, when applied to Satan, has been exaggerated over the centuries. The ultimate demon took on a forked tongue, cloven hooves, reptilian skin, bat's wings, talons, red skin, and a hairy body.

It is said that Satan travels back and forth between earth and hell. Aboveground, he rules wicked politicians, brings sickness and death to humanity, and uses his powers to masquerade as a good angel. In hell, Satan is said to oversee a bizarre, gruesome chamber of horrors where the impious forever burn in a sea of fire.

## Demon in Grandma's Clothing

Just as millions claim to have had angelic encounters, numerous people say they have met up with Satan or his minions. Sometimes these visits are short but frightening encounters, other times the victims must fight off the demon for extended periods. Oftentimes the visits are inexplicable, and the observer has no idea why the demon appeared. In 2004 Sarah L. described on the Paranormal Phenomena Web site a brief brush with a fallen angel.

Sarah says she was eight years old when she observed her grandmother taking things from her bedroom or moving things around and messing up the room. Sarah asked her to stop. The grandmother responded by saying she had no idea what Sarah was talking about. One day, Sarah left school early and caught

*This French engraving shows Pan, the Greek god of Nature. Since the Middle Ages, Satan has been portrayed as similar to Pan and is said to have a human head and torso with the hind legs, ears, and horns of a goat.*

grandma in the act, staring into her closet in an unusual manner. The young girl yelled at her grandmother to stop but the older women kept staring into the closet. Sarah continues the story:

> Suddenly, she turned her head slowly toward me and gave me the coldest look ever! She had the most evil eyes I had ever seen! A chill ran up and down my spine! Those were not my grandma's eyes, I thought. Then she looked away from me and walked into my closet! . . . But when I went to my closet . . . she was gone! I froze for a few seconds![29]

Sarah called for her grandmother, and the woman answered from the kitchen. Sarah realized that the creature disguised as her grandmother was really a demon who was visiting her room. She offers no explanation or reason for this demonic visitation.

## The Little Red Devil

Sometimes when demons appear they are more obvious than the one that visited Sarah. This was the case with Charlie, a devout Christian and Baptist deacon from Middlesboro, Kentucky. According to an account on the Paranormal Phenomena Web site, Charlie did not believe in supernatural phenomena until his encounter with a creature under his house.

Charlie's home was built over a crawl space that had a dirt floor which needed to be cleaned periodically. Charlie was under the house one day, on his hands and knees sweeping up brush and leaves, when he noticed a large rock over by the edge of the crawlspace that had never been there before. He was puzzled and struggled to move the rock. Beneath it he saw a small, round hole, a tunnel that seemed to lead into an underground world.

Charlie got a flashlight and was peering into the tunnel when he heard something running toward him. Suddenly a small red being emerged from the hole. It had a long tail, pointed ears, and pawlike hands with fingers. The creature glared angrily at Charlie, stomped its feet, hissed, and spat a foul juice into his face. As quickly as it appeared, the creature returned to the hole, leaving Charlie too stunned to move for a moment. Finally, gathering his wits, he ran to the garage, mixed up some cement, and filled in the hole. The demon never reappeared, but Charlie never forgot his encounter with what he called his Little Red Devil.

## The Fallen Angel

Some demonic encounters have much more serious consequences than Charlie's. A man named Richard reported that he was walking in the woods with a friend when he noticed complete silence. No birds chirped, no leaves rustled, and no breeze was blowing.

Richard, writing of his experience on the Paranormal Phenomena Web site, says his friend unexpectedly fell to the ground and could not move. It was as if he were bolted to the ground or held down by some sort of supernatural magnetic force. As Richard struggled to pick up his friend, he noticed a large, dark figure, about 7 feet (2m) tall, standing close by. Richard continues the story:

> The thing looked at me and just stood there star-
> ing for a moment. I felt a heavy presence of disgust

and hate. It seemed to grow stronger as I looked at him. I broke eye contact with him, not wanting to feel those emotions too much longer, but he spoke to me in a clear voice. He commanded me to look at him. I knew that he was evil and I shouldn't look, but I wasn't afraid of what he was so I did anyway. . . . He wore all black and had enormous wings. But they weren't like a bird's, they were strange wings. One wing was only thin bones, like those that make up a bat's wing. And the other was a wing of rotting flesh and molting feathers. The only way I can title him in appearance was like a fallen angel.[30]

The fallen angel commanded Richard to bow to him and promised he would return someday. Richard refused to bow, and the demon forced him to the ground and said, "Don't forget your debt with the devil."[31] Richard felt a torturous stabbing pain as the devil laughed and walked away. Suddenly, his friend got up off the ground, acting as if nothing had happened. He just saw Richard freeze in his tracks for a moment. Although his friend remembered nothing, Richard noticed the trees nearby were burned and the ground was cracked and dusty. The trees have not grown back to this day, and Richard lives in fear that the devil will return someday to collect his debt.

## Witches and Devils

Richard had no idea why a fallen angel chose to cross his path. However, some people intentionally seek out Satan. Contact is made through rituals in which the individual uses prayer to call

# The Cursed Realm of Fallen Angels

I n ancient Christian literature such as The Apocalypse of Peter, writers let their imaginations run wild
when describing hell. In *Four Views of Hell* theologian
William V. Crockett lists some of the torments carried
out by Satan and his princes in the cursed realm of fall-
en angels:

> [We] find blasphemers hanging by their
> tongues. Adulterous women who [braid-
> ed] their hair to entice men dangle over

up Satan or one of his minions, such as Mephistopheles, from hell.
Oftentimes those conducting such ceremonies do not believe
that Satan is the pure evil being depicted in the Bible. They think
that he can grant them supernatural powers that can be used to
further their personal desires.

boiling mire by their necks or hair. Slan-derers chew their tongues, hot irons burn their eyes. Other evildoers suffer in equally picturesque ways. Murderers are cast into pits filled with venomous reptiles, and worms fill their bodies. . . . Those who chatted idly during church stand in a pool of burning sulphur and pitch [tar]. Idolaters are driven up cliffs by demons where they plunge to the rocks below, only to be driven up again. Those who turned their backs on God are turned and baked slowly in the fires of hell.

William Crockett, ed., *Four Views of Hell.* Grand Rapids, MI: Zondervan, 1992, pp. 46–47.

In past centuries witches were widely believed to have obtained their powers from Satan. By conducting ghastly ceremonies they were able call forth the devil and pledge their souls to him. One such ritual, which allegedly took place in 1611, is described by German theologian Philip Ludwig Elich:

The whole foul mob and stinkard rabble sing the most obscene ... and abominable songs in honor of the Devil. One witch yells *Harr, harr* a second hag, Devil, Devil; jump hither, jump thither; a third, Gambol [leap] hither, gambol thither.... And so the wild [ceremony] waxes frantic what time the bedlam rout are screeching, hissing, howling, caterwauling, and whooping lewd [salutations to Satan].[32]

Witches were said to have magical powers after they communed with Satan. They were able to cast spells, fly through the air on broomsticks, become invisible, and control people, animals, weather, and other aspects of the natural world.

## The Devil's Contract

Many stories about witches and devils from the distant past are exaggerated or simply made up. And the witch hysteria that swept across Europe in the seventeenth century resulted in the torture and execution of thousands of innocent people, the majority of them women. Nonetheless it remains a widely held notion that anyone who endeavors to make a contract with the devil does so at the peril of losing his or her eternal soul. And many stories are told about those who had extremely negative experiences after purportedly making a pact with Satan.

One of the earliest stories about the devil's contract was written in the fourth century. In A.D. 353, St. Basil, who lived in what is now Turkey, told the story of a young slave who traded his soul to the devil for the love of his master's daughter.

In later years, a farm girl named Elizabeth Styles was put on trial for her pact with the devil. In 1664 she claimed that Satan appeared to her as either a handsome young man or a black dog. In *A History of the Devil* William Wood describes Styles's encounter with the king of the fallen angels:

> He promised her that for 12 years she should have money, live gallantly, and enjoy the pleasures of the world if she would sign a contract in her own blood, agreeing to give him her soul and observe his laws. . . . So he had pricked the fourth finger of her right hand (the scar was still visible), and with a drop or two of blood she had signed the paper with an O. Upon this, the devil had given her sixteen pence [about $20] and disappeared.[33]

It might be understandable why a destitute slave boy or a poor farm girl would enter into a contract with Satan. However, even wealthy, educated men have been charged with making deals with the devil. For example, at least 3 priests were accused of selling their souls to Satan in order to be named pope. They include eleventh-century French scholar Sylvester II, thirteenth-century Portuguese priest John XXI, and fifteenth-century Italian pope Gregory XII.

## Your Soul Will Belong to Me

One of the most well-known pacts with the devil in recent times concerns seminal blues musician Robert Johnson. It is said that

*This woodcut shows a sorcerer and a witch casting spells. Witches were said to have magical powers after they communed with Satan.*

Johnson met up with the devil at a crossroads south of Rosedale, Mississippi, around 1931. Johnson was an unknown guitar player who was so bad he was rebuked by blues legend Son House who said, "Put that guitar down, boy, you drivin' people nuts."[34]

Dejected, penniless, and in need of a drink, Johnson was walking down the lonely Highway 8 with his guitar slung over his shoulder. Where the highway crossed Dockery Road, Johnson saw a sick dog moaning in the ditch and a strange man sitting on a log. The man told Johnson he was late for his appointment, and the frightened blues player fell down on his knees. The story is continued by Rosedale resident Henry Goodman, who relates his version of Johnson's meeting with the fallen angel:

> [The devil said:] Stand up, Robert Johnson. You want to throw that guitar over there in that ditch . . . because you just another guitar player like all the rest, or you want to play that guitar like nobody ever played it before? Make a sound nobody ever heard before? You want to be the King of the Delta Blues and have all the whiskey and women you want?[35]

As the devil finished talking, Johnson saw the moon growing bigger and bigger until he felt it searing his neck like the summer noonday sun. Meanwhile the moaning of the dog penetrated every nerve in Johnson's body until he could feel it vibrating in his heart and shaking his entire being. This caused the strings of Johnson's guitar to vibrate in a soulful and darkly beautiful melody. Johnson then had an out-of-body experience. Floating

**QUOTE**

"The whole foul mob and stinkard rabble sing the most obscene . . . and abominable songs in honor of the Devil."

—German theologian Philip Ludwig Elich describing a seventeenth-century ceremony where witches called up the devil.

above the scene, the bluesman realized the dog was a hellhound working for the devil.

Finally the bluesman answered the devil's question. "I got to have that sound, Devil-Man. That sound is mine. Where do I sign?" The devil says,

Your word is good enough. All you got to do is keep walking north. But you better be prepared. There are consequences. . . . You are going to have the Blues like never known to this world. My left hand will be forever wrapped around your soul, and your music will possess all who hear it. That's what's going to happen. That's what you better be prepared for. Your soul will belong to me. Go on, Robert Johnson. You the King of the Delta Blues."[36]

Johnson did go on to achieve fame with an epic combination of singing, guitar playing, and songwriting skills. The albums he recorded between 1937 and 1938 produced songs that influenced some of the biggest names in rock and roll, including Bob Dylan, Jimi Hendrix, the Beatles, the Rolling Stones, Eric Clapton, and Led Zeppelin. However, Johnson met his end in 1938 at a country crossroad not much different than the one where he was rumored to have met the devil.

Johnson was only 27 when he died. Some say he was poisoned by his lover's jealous husband, others say he died of syphilis. But to this day, residents of the Mississippi Delta region claim that when Johnson died, the devil was simply taking his due and collecting the soul the guitar player had signed away many years before.

Skeptics doubt it is possible to sell one's soul to the devil. As with heavenly angels, proof that devils are real does not exist. But that has not slowed a widespread belief in Lucifer, who fell from heaven like a shooting star falls through the sky at midnight. And just as day follows night, the dark deeds of the fallen angels will forever contrast with the luminous light of good angels. It is a heroic battle as old as humanity and will doubtless continue as long as the moon follows the sun in the sky.

# NOTES

### Introduction: Attracted to Angels

1. Quoted in Rex Hauck, ed., *Angels: The Mysterious Messengers*. New York: Ballantine, 1994, p. 5.

### Chapter 1: In the Beginning

2. Quoted in Angelight, "Ancient Angel History," March 2000. http://members.aol.com

3. Quoted in Sivasiva Palani, "New Angels on Angels," Hinduism Today, 2008. www.hinduismtoday.com.

4. Palani, "New Angels on Angels."

### Chapter 2: The Lives of Angels

5. David Keck, *Angels and Angelology in the Middle Ages*. Oxford: Oxford University Press, 1998, p. 29.

6. Quoted in Steven Chase, ed., *Angelic Spirituality*. New York: Paulist Press, 2002, pp. 151–52.

7. Plato, "Phaedrus," Internet Classics Archive, 2008. http://classics.mit.edu.

8. Quoted in Believe, "Christian Halo, Nimbus," September 2, 2007. http://mb-soft.com.

9. Janice T. Connell, *Angel Power*. New York: Ballantine, 1995, p. 12.

10. Timothy Snodgrass, "Visions of California," End Time Prophetic Vision, June 18, 2005. www.etpv.org.

11. Quoted in Joan Wester Anderson, *Where Miracles Happen*. New York: Ballantine, 1994, pp. 26–27.

12. Quoted in Brad Steiger and Sherry Hansen Steiger, *Angels over Their Shoulders*. New York: Fawcett Columbine, 1995, p. 35.

13. Joan Wester Anderson, *Where Angels Walk*. New York: Ballantine, 1992, p. 141.

14. Quoted in St. Thomas Aquinas, "Question 50. The Substance of the Angels Absolutely Considered," New Advent, 2007. www.newadvent.org.

15. Quoted in Billy Graham, *Angels:*

*God's Secret Agents.* Dallas: Word, 1994, p. v.

## Chapter 3: Angel Encounters

16. Quoted in Paranormal Phenomena, "Encounters with Angels," March 15, 2008. http://paranormal.about.com.
17. Eileen Elias Freeman, *Touched by Angels.* New York: Warner, 1993, p. 46.
18. Quoted in Paranormal Phenomena, "Encounters with Angels."
19. Quoted in Steiger and Steiger, *Angels over Their Shoulders,* pp. 24–25.
20. Quoted in Steiger and Steiger, *Angels over Their Shoulders,* p. 25.
21. Quoted in Steiger and Steiger, *Angels over Their Shoulders,* p. 25.
22. Quoted in P.M.H. Atwater, "Childhood Near-Death Experiences," Near Death Experiences and the Afterlife, November 21, 2006. www.near-death.com.
23. Quoted in Atwater, "Childhood Near-Death Experiences."
24. Silver Raven Wolf, *Angels: Companions in Magick.* St. Paul: Llewellyn, 2003, p. x.
25. Quoted in Wolf, *Angels: Companions in Magick,* p. 102.

## Chapter 4: Fallen Angels

26. Lynn Picknett, *The Secret History of Lucifer.* New York: Carroll & Graf, 2005, p. 14.
27. Quoted in WhiteRose's Garden, "Adramelech," 2007. www.whiterosesgarden.com.
28. Quoted in Montague Summers, *The History of Witchcraft.* New York: Carol, 1993, p. 82.
29. Sarah L., "Demon in Grandma's Clothing," Paranormal Phenomena. February 2004. http://paranormal.about.com.
30. Richard, "Fallen Angel," Paranormal Phenomena, March 2005. http://paranormal.about.com.
31. Quoted in Richard, "Fallen Angel."
32. Quoted in Summers, *The History of Witchcraft,* p. 148.
33. William Wood, *A History of the Devil.* New York: G.P. Putnam's Sons, 1974, p. 196.
34. Quoted in Rolf Potts, "Robert Johnson Sold His Soul to the Devil in Rosedale, Mississippi," Vagablogging, April 16, 2004. www.vagablogging.net.
35. Quoted in Potts, "Robert Johnson Sold His Soul."
36. Quoted in Potts, "Robert Johnson Sold His Soul."

# FOR FURTHER RESEARCH

## Books

Miriam Chaikin, *Angel Secrets: Stories Based on Jewish Legend.* New York: Henry Holt, 2005. Six stories told with imagination and humor about the angelic links between heaven and Earth according to Jewish teachings.

Glennyce S. Eckersley, *Teen Angel: True Stories of Teenage Experiences of Angels.* London: Trafalgar Square, 2007. A collection of stories about angelic encounters between angels and teenagers, including miraculous lifesaving intervention.

Claire Llewellyn, *Saints and Angels.* Boston: Kingfisher, 2003. Descriptions of different kinds of angels, profiles of three specific angels, and information about archangels.

Patricia D. Netzley, *Angels.* San Diego, CA: Lucent, 2001. A study of angelic belief throughout history, stories of angelic encounters, and information about fallen angels and demons.

Silver Raven Wolf, *Angels: Companions in Magick.* St. Paul, MN: Llewellyn, 2003. A view of angels, angelic interference, and angel encounters from a New Age perspective.

## Web Sites

**Angel History** (www.fortunecity.com/millennium/rover/120/aglhis.html). A Fortune City site containing information about angel beliefs, hierarchies, and names with links to angel art, poetry, and quotes.

**Encounters with Angels** (http://paranormal.about.com/od/angels/a/aa032408.htm). A Paranormal Phenomena Web site with hundreds of stories concerning purported real-life encounters with angels written by volunteer contributors who experienced the event.

**Hierarchy Angels, an Overview Chart**

of the Angelic Hierarchy, Nine Choirs, Triads (www.angel-guide.com/hierarchy-angels.html). A site provided by Angel Guide that describes the nine choirs of angels, each divided into triads.

Strange and Supernatural: Phantom Encounters (www.geocities.com/strange-supernatural/phantom_encounters.htm). A Web site with purported photographs of angels, ghosts, and other supernatural phenomena along with explanations of the situation in which the photo was taken.

Your True Tales: Demon Encounters (http://paranormal.about.com/library/bltales_demons.htm). Allegedly true stories sent in to this Paranormal Phenomena site by those who have encountered fallen angels. Titles of stories include "Battle with a Demon," "Demonic Prank," and "Don't Dare the Devil."

# INDEX

# ABOUT THE AUTHOR

Stuart A. Kallen is a prolific author who has written more than 250 nonfiction books for children and young adults over the past 20 years. His books have covered countless aspects of human history, culture, and science from the building of the pyramids to the music of the twentyfirst century. Some of his recent titles include *History of World Music, Romantic Art,* and *Women of the Civil Rights Movement.* Kallen is also an accomplished singer-songwriter and guitarist in San Diego, California.